THAT'S WHAT GRANDMOTHERS ARE FOR

ARLENE USLANDER

CHICAGO SPECTRUM PRESS

CHICAGO SPECTRUM PRESS
1571 SHERMAN AVE, ANNEX C
EVANSTON, IL 60201
800-594-5190

Printed in the U.S.A.

10 9 8 7 6 5 4 3 2 1

ISBN: 1-886094-13-6

Cover Illustration by Judy Flores

To Eric, Ryan, Carly,
and all the grandchildren,
everywhere,
who have such a special place
in their grandmothers' hearts.

You were ten minutes old when I met you
on that very special day.
Mom and Dad were so glad,
and they asked me,
"So what does Grandma say?"

I told them I'd never, not ever
seen such a fine baby before.
And I quietly said (as I kissed your sweet head),
"After all, **that's what grandmas are for!"**

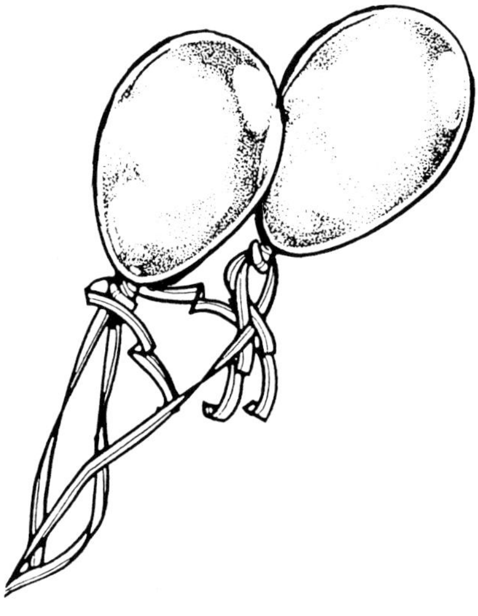

When you finally came home to your nursery,
you fretted and cried all night long.
Your Father, was worried;
your Mother, worn out.
They were sure they had done something wrong!

When I asked them if I could just hold you,
your Mom said, "*Please*, give it a try,"
so I lifted you out of your cradle,
and sang you a soft lullaby.
I walked and I talked and I rocked you
'til you finally closed your eyes.

Mother was grateful; Father, amazed,
as I carefully closed Baby's door.
I wasn't surprised, for I truly believe
that's what a grandma is for.

When I was asked to babysit,
I was happy as could be.
The first time we were all alone—
what a wonderful treat for me!

I watched you sleep so peacefully
and stroked your precious hair.
Before very long, I dozed off, too,
just sitting in my chair.

But I heard you cry, so I went to see
what the matter could be.
Then you just cooed, as if to say,
"I'm glad you're here with me."

I picked you up and held you close,
behind your nursery door.
The night was cold, but I kept you warm.
(That's what grandmothers are for.)

"You are going to spoil our little one,"
your parents said to me,
"if you keep cuddling and rocking,
and holding our child on your knee."

"Now listen here!" I said to them,
as I *loudly* closed their door.
"Hasn't anybody told you
that's what grandmothers are for?"

You were the cutest baby
(of course, the smartest, too).
I proudly showed your pictures
to everyone I knew.

I talked about you *all the time.*
Was I an awful bore?
Perhaps—but after all, you know,
that's what grandmothers are for.

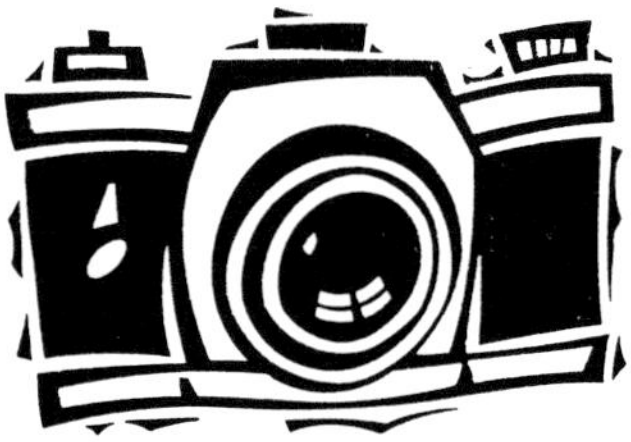

When your Mom and Dad were both at work,
you spent the days with me.
We liked to picnic in the park;
so much to do and see.

I pushed you in the baby swing;
your eyes filled with delight!
You held my sleeve and scampered down
the shiny, slippery slide.

When a naughty child threw dirt at you,
I said, “Don’t do that anymore!”
You were only two,
yet you smiled like you knew
that’s what grandmothers are for.

On a warm, clear day, we went to the beach.
You tried to eat the sand.
You waded in the water
clinging tightly to my hand.

We found a pretty starfish that
we threw back in the sea.
You waved to a big brown pelican
as he landed in a tree.

Then you stubbed your toe on a pointy rock,
and your little foot was sore.
I kissed the "ouch" to make it go 'way.
(That's what grandmothers are for.)

I went with you to nursery school
and listened as you said,
you didn't want to sing or dance,
and then you stood on your head.

When Teacher passed out cookies,
you threw yours on the floor.
I still thought you the best in class.
(That's what grandmothers are for.)

We went for a walk before bedtime
and tried to count the stars.
We sang a tune
to the man-in-the-moon,
but we didn't get very far.

"I'm too cold and too little," you said to me.
"I can't walk anymore."
So I picked you up and carried you.
(That's what Grandmothers are for.)

Whenever your folks went out at night,
and you and I were home,
you tiptoed to my room and said,
"I don't want to sleep alone."

I put you in my great big bed;
then I gently closed the door.
We snuggled close, as warm as toast.
(That's what grandmothers are for.)

One day you had the sneezes,
and your voice was very hoarse.
I made you a cup of hot chocolate,
with marshmallows, of course.

I read you 14 stories,
but still you wanted more.
I read to you 'til *my* voice was hoarse.
(That's what grandmothers are for.)

"Do you love me, Grandma?"
You asked one night.
"Do I *love* you?" I said.
(Is a polar bear white?)

"I love you more
than all the stars in the sky.
"And I love you more
than all the times you ask 'Why?'"

"Even more," you asked,
"than *all* the toys in the stores?"
"Oh, a zillion times more!"
(That's what grandmas are for.)

We visited the zoo in May,
you liked the monkeys best.
You stroked a baby rabbit,
and saw ducklings in their nest.

You said to a talking parrot,
"I'm four. How old are you?"
He kept saying, "Hello! Hello!
My name is Buster Blue!"

You didn't look very happy
when you heard a lion roar.
I said, "My dear, you're safe with me.
That's what grandmothers are for."

One day it was raining very hard;
you couldn't go anywhere.
I helped you make a tent in your room;
we ate our lunch in there.

We looked at old family pictures
'til sunshine striped the floor.
Then I taught you a song to welcome the sun.
(That's what grandmothers are for.)

I baked you special cookies;
I made you pizza, too—
all the things you love to eat,
and then when I was through,
I let you choose your favorites
at the corner grocery store.
My grandma let me do that, too.
(That's what grandmothers are for.)

You broke your very favorite toy,
A penguin that did tricks.
He wouldn't do a single thing;
you said, "He must be sick!"

But while you slept, "Dr. Grandma"
fixed him up for you,
and when you woke, he did his tricks
just as good as new.

"You fixed him, Gram!" you said to me.
"He's not broken anymore."
"Why, naturally!" I said and winked.
"That's what grandmothers are for!"

When you were six, I went to school
to see you in a play.
You were supposed to be a maple tree
and had no lines to say.

You stood so still, so straight and tall,
I clapped and yelled, "Encore!"
You smiled and waved, as if to say,
"That's what grandmothers are for!"

You and your Dad were at my house
one Sunday afternoon.
Dad looked at all the toys and games
I kept in every room.

"As many toys *here* as home?" asked Dad.
"And maybe even *more?*"
"Could be," I said, "but everyone knows
that's what grandma's house is for."

I remember how your first tooth came out
when you bit into a plum.
You lost another in a piece
of yellow bubble gum.

You put them under your pillow,
but you wouldn't turn out the light,
so the shy little tooth fairy
didn't come that night.

But Grandma left two dollars
(or perhaps a little more...?)
Your parents said I gave too much.
(That's what grandmothers are for.)

You and I went fishing
in the pond across the way.
You'd never caught a fish before,
though you did catch one that day.

But when you reeled it in, you said,
"This fish is just a baby.
Do you think its mommy will be sad?"
"I don't know," I said—"well, maybe."

"Let's put it back," you said to me.
"We won't fish anymore."
I told you I knew just how you felt.
(That's what grandmothers are for.)

I was feeling very sad one night;
my best friend had moved away.
It was hard to get my face to smile;
there wasn't much to say.

You brought *me* milk and cookies;
then you gently closed the door.
"Don't be sad," you said. "You still have me."
(That's what GRANDCHILDREN are for.)